BOLTON LIBRARIES

BT 099 8302 3

I0229424

BOLTON LIBRARIES CHILDREN'S SERVICES	
BT 1091133 2	
PETERS	02-May-02
J941.01MID	£10.50
ᴚm	

ROMANS, ANGLO-SAXONS & VIKINGS IN BRITAIN

HAYDN MIDDLETON

H www.heinemann.co.uk
Visit our website to find out more information about Heinemann books.

To order:
☎ Phone 44 (0) 1865 888020
📄 Send a fax to 44 (0) 1865 314091
💻 Visit the Heinemann Bookshop at www.heinemann.co.uk to browse our catalogue and order online.

First published in Great Britain by Heinemann Library, Halley Court, Jordan Hill, Oxford OX2 8EJ, a division of Reed Educational and Professional Publishing Ltd. Heinemann is a registered trademark of Reed Educational & Professional Publishing Ltd.

OXFORD MELBOURNE AUCKLAND JOHANNESBURG BLANTYRE
GABORONE IBADAN PORTSMOUTH (NH) USA CHICAGO

© Reed Educational and Professional Publishing Ltd 2001
The moral right of the proprietor has been asserted.

All rights reserved. No part of this publication may be reproduced, stored in a retrieval system, or transmitted in any form or by any means, electronic, mechanical, photocopying, recording, or otherwise without either the prior written permission of the Publishers or a licence permitting restricted copying in the United Kingdom issued by the Copyright Licensing Agency Ltd, 90 Tottenham Court Road, London W1P 0LP.

Designed by Celia Floyd
Illustrations by Jeff Edwards
Originated by Dot Gradations
Printed in Italy by LEGO

05 04 03 02 01   05 04 03 02 01
10 9 8 7 6 5 4 3 2 1   10 9 8 7 6 5 4 3 2 1
ISBN 0 431 10200 7 (hardback)   ISBN 0 431 10209 0 (paperback)

British Library Cataloguing in Publication Data

Middleton, Haydn
  Romans, Anglo-Saxons and Vikings in Britain. – (Exploring History)
  1.Romans – Great Britain 2.Vikings – Great Britain 3.Anglo Saxons – Great Britain
  4.Great Britain – History – To 1066
  I. Title
  941'.01

Acknowledgements

The Publishers would like to thank the following for permission to reproduce photographs:
Ancient Art and Architecture: pg.14; Art Archive: pg.22; Bath and North East Somerset Council: pg.5; British Museum: pg.12, pg.13, pg.18, pg.19; Corbis: pg.10; pg.11; pg.15, pg.16, pg.21, pg.26, pg.29; Dorset County Council 2000: Hulton: pg.27; pg.8; John Seely: pg.9; Richard Alexander Clarke: pg.6; Sally & Richard Greenhill: pg.4; Tracy Griffiths & Magnet Harlequin: pg.17; Werner Forman: pg.23, pg.25; York Archaeological Trust: pg.28.

Cover photograph reproduced with permission of the British Library.

Every effort has been made to contact copyright holders of any material reproduced in this book. Any omissions will be rectified in subsequent printings if notice is given to the Publisher.

Any words appearing in the text in bold, **like this**, are explained in the glossary.

Contents

Why do people move away from where they
were born?   4

Who invaded and settled in Britain a long time ago?   6

A Roman case study

How do we know about the Romans and Celts?   8

Who was Boudicca?   10

What happened in AD 60?   12

How did the Romans change Britain when they
    settled here?   14

An Anglo-Saxon case study

How was the grave at Sutton Hoo discovered?   18

What was life like at the time the person in the
    grave was alive?   20

What have we found out about who was buried
    in the Sutton Hoo grave?   22

A Viking case study

Why did the Vikings travel from their homelands and
    where did they go?   24

When did the Vikings come to Britain to raid and to stay? 26

What evidence is there that the Vikings settled in Britain? 28

Timeline   30

Glossary   31

Index   32

Why do people move away from where they were born?

Have you always lived in Britain? Have you always lived in the same part of Britain? Or did you come here from a different country? If you move from one country to another, that is called **emigrating**. A new person in a country is called an **immigrant**.

Britain is a country of many cultures now.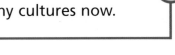

Why do people emigrate?

Think of the footballer Gianfranco Zola. He is Italian, but he was transferred to a club in Britain: Chelsea. So he moved from Italy to Britain. He brought his family, and they all became immigrants. Lots of other people come to Britain for jobs. Some stay for just a short time; others settle in Britain with their families and never leave. These people have all *chosen* to emigrate.

Fleeing to safety

Some people *have* to emigrate. Think of the **refugees** who came to Britain from Kosovo. They came here because they were suffering terribly in their home country. If there is a war where you live, then you may feel you need to escape to somewhere safer. As a **citizen** of a new country, you can try to make a fresh start.

Invaders and conquerors

Over the centuries, another sort of people have come here from other countries. They were armies of invaders. They conquered Britain, or parts of Britain, then lived here themselves. In this book, you can find out about three groups of invaders: the Romans, the Anglo-Saxons and the Vikings.

 Bath

These are the famous baths at the Roman health resort of Bath, in Somerset. They were built over local hot springs, which people thought could cure diseases. The Romans called Bath 'Aquae Sulis' after Sul, a British goddess of the area. Even in towns where there were no springs, the Romans set up bath-houses.

 Exploring further

The Heinemann Explore CD-ROM will give you information about people who invaded and settled in Britain in the past. From the Contents screen you can click on the blue words to find out about the Romans, Anglo-Saxons and Vikings.

Who invaded and settled in Britain a long time ago?

In the year AD 43, a war began in Britain. On one side were the **Celtic tribes** who lived here. On the other were the invading armies of the Roman **Empire**. Britain was rich in corn and cattle, and in minerals like silver and iron. So it was well worth conquering. But some of the British tribes fought hard against the invaders.

The conquest begins

First the Romans conquered the south-east corner of Britain. Then they marched further north and west. As the Romans advanced, they built forts and roads. Soldiers in the forts kept the conquered lands under control. The roads helped them to travel quickly to trouble-spots. Soon most of southern Britain came under Roman control.

Roman defences

The Romans built forts like Burgh Castle on the east coast to protect Britain from Anglo-Saxon raiders.

After the conquest, the Romans settle

The Romans settled mainly in the south. They called this **province** of the Empire 'Britannia'. They ruled over it for nearly four hundred years following this. Often they brought their families to live with them, and settled alongside the Celtic people.

100 BC	
55 BC	Julius Caesar leads expedition to Britain
0	Roman invasion of Britain
AD 43	
AD 60	Boudicca's revolt
AD 100	
AD 200	
AD 300	
AD 400	
AD 410	Anglo-Saxons begin to invade Britain
	Britain no longer part of Roman Empire
AD 500	
AD 600	
c. AD 624	Ship burial at Sutton Hoo
AD 700	
AD 793	Vikings attack Lindisfarne
AD 800	
AD 900	
AD 1000	
	Norman invasion of Britain
AD 1066	
AD 1100	

A new threat

In AD 793, raiders attacked the **monastery** at Lindisfarne, a small island off the north-east coast of England. They were Vikings from Scandinavia. Travelling by land as well as by sea, these Vikings terrorized a vast part of the world for about 300 years. In some places, including England, they settled and mixed in with the native people.

Invaders from the east

As other parts of the Roman Empire needed protecting, fewer troops were kept in Britain. Sea-raiders from Europe took advantage of this and launched attack after attack. Some brought their families and settled in Britain. Some of these invaders were Angles, some were Saxons, others were Jutes, Franks or Frisians. We call them all Anglo-Saxons. After a while, the settlers started calling themselves 'Englisc'. From that came the word for the country – 'England' and the people 'English'.

Exploring further – Invaders and warriors

Writings that survive from the time tell us what the people of Britain thought of the invaders. Follow this path on the CD-ROM to find out what we have been told about Anglo-Saxon warriors:

Anglo-Saxons in Britain > Written Sources > Anglo-Saxon Warriors.

How do we know about the Romans and Celts?

The Romans wrote books about Roman history and the Roman way of life. But the **tribes** of **Celtic Britons** left no books. We have to rely on Roman writings to know what British life was like. We can also look at old British things that **archaeologists** have found.

Multi-purpose hillforts

A Roman geographer and historian called Strabo wrote about what he saw of Britain. 'Their cities are the forests, for they cut down trees, and fence in large circles of land. Inside, they build huts, and pen in their cattle for short periods.' These places that Strabo describes were called **hillforts**.

The Romans lived in towns with paved streets, public baths and theatres, not in hillforts or villages like the Celts. They wrote and spoke in **Latin** instead of the 'barbarian' Celtic languages.

Hillforts

Hillforts were market places for trade, centres of worship, and places of defence. This is Maiden Castle in Dorset.

Britons

Julius Caesar made two visits to Britain, in 55 BC and 54 BC. He wrote about what he found.

By far the most civilised natives are those living in Kent. All the Britons dye their bodies with **woad**. This makes them go all blue, so that they look more terrifying in battle.

What the Celts believed

The Celts worshipped many different gods and spirits. The Celtic priests, called **Druids**, set down rules on how to do this. The **deities** could be lurking in all kinds of holy places: forest groves, rivers or even oddly shaped rocks or trees. Archaeologists still find offerings, like carved animals, cups or weapons, which people left for these gods and spirits.

What the Romans believed

Romans worshipped many different gods too: gods who watched over each home, gods who were the spirits of dead relatives, and gods like Jupiter, that everyone worshipped.

Pompeii

The town of Pompeii, in Italy, was buried by a volcanic eruption in AD 79. It has been well preserved. Pompeii shows us that Roman towns were very different to the Celts' hillforts.

Exploring further – What the Romans believed

To find out what the Romans believed follow this path on the CD-ROM:
Romans in Britain > Exploring > Beliefs > The gods of Roman Britain
You can also discover more about Celtic beliefs:
Romans in Britain > Exploring > Beliefs > Old Gods and Druids.

Who was Boudicca?

Boudicca was a **Celtic** queen. She was married to the king of the Iceni **tribe**, who lived in East Anglia. In AD 60, after her husband died, Boudicca led a great revolt against Britain's new Roman rulers. This revolt made her one of the most famous women in British history.

Boudicca was a powerful and determined warrior and leader. Even so, at a great battle in the Midlands, the Celtic **Britons** were crushed. Dio wrote that 'Boudicca then became ill and died'. Tacitus wrote that Boudicca poisoned herself.

What Dio wrote

Dio was a historian who lived around the year AD 200. He described Boudicca: *'She was a woman of the British royal family who had great intelligence … She was very tall and grim; her gaze was sharp and her voice was harsh; she grew her auburn hair down to her hips and wore a large golden **torque** and a big patterned cloak with a thick plaid fastened over it.'*

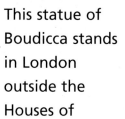

Celtic queen

This statue of Boudicca stands in London outside the Houses of Parliament.

Fighting the Celts

This tombstone comes from Colchester. It was put up before Boudicca's revolt. It shows a Roman figure on horseback, probably the soldier in the tomb, making a native Briton cringe under him.

What Tacitus wrote

Tacitus was a Roman historian who lived soon after Boudicca's time. He wrote about what she did before battle: *'Boudicca drove round all the tribes in a chariot with her daughters in front of her. "We British are used to women commanders in war," she cried. "But I am not fighting for my kingdom and wealth. I am fighting as an ordinary person for my freedom… The gods will help us! … Think of how many of you are fighting – and why. Then you will win this battle, or die."*

Caratacus

Caratacus was king of the Celtic Catuvellauni tribe. He fought hard against the Roman invasion that began in AD 43. After he was defeated in southern Britain, he fled to the west to fight on. After another defeat, he escaped to the northern lands of the Brigantes tribe, but their queen, Cartimandua, handed him over to the invaders. He was sent in chains to Rome, where he lived for the rest of his life.

Exploring further – Cartimandua

Not all Celts reacted to the Roman invaders in the same way as Boudicca.
Follow this path to read about the life of Cartimandua:
Romans in Britain > Biographies > Cartimandua

What happened in AD 60?

Some British **tribes** gave in to the Romans without fighting. They hoped to get rewards by being friendly with them. Other tribes fought hard to resist the Romans. In AD 58 the Emperor sent a new **Governor**, Suetonius Paulinus to launch a big campaign against the rebel tribes in the west. By AD 60 he had been very successful. But back in East Anglia, the previously friendly Iceni had risen in revolt.

What was bugging Boudicca?

The king of the Iceni had just died. At once the Romans **plundered** his household and lands, and badly mistreated his family. The king's widow Boudicca decided to take vengeance – and **Britons** from other tribes flocked to support her. They felt that the Romans treated them like slaves. Their revolt was a terrible thing. They headed for Colchester, London and St Albans, three of the largest towns built by the Romans. Then they utterly destroyed them.

Rebellion

Colchester was ruthlessly attacked by the rebels. The head of the statue of the Emperor Claudius from the temple was found in the River Alde in Suffolk in 1907.

12

Weaponry

We can learn about the Roman army from the weapons that are found.

Roman revenge

Paulinus rushed his troops back from the west. They clashed with Boudicca's army in the middle of southern Britain. 'The struggle took many forms,' wrote the historian Dio. 'Light-armed troops from both sides fought. **Cavalry** charged cavalry, while the Roman archers fired at the barbarian chariots… Equal bravery was shown on both sides.' But at last the British rebels were crushed. About 80,000 of them were killed.

After the revolt, thousands more Roman troops were sent to Britain. They took terrible revenge on the tribes who had rebelled. This must have made some Britons hate their Roman rulers even more.

The Romans did bring peace though, and Britain stayed part of the Roman **Empire** for another 350 years. The Romans built roads, towns and **villas**. Some top Britons shared in the comforts and wealth that this brought. For most of the time the Romans also made sure that peace reigned. It was far easier for them to govern a peaceful Britain.

Exploring further – Boudicca's revolt

The Digging Deeper section of the CD-ROM allows you to find out more about Boudicca's revolt. Follow this path:
Romans in Britain > Digging Deeper > The Roman Conquest of Britain > The great revolt

How did the Romans change Britain when they settled here?

Before the Roman conquest, the nearest things the Britons had to towns were **hillforts**. The Romans believed in towns and cities as centres for government, trade, worship and entertainment. And by building them in new **provinces**, they could serve as models of the Roman way of life. Some towns in Britain were built for Roman soldiers to retire to. Others grew up through trade, or were built on the strongholds of the old **Celtic tribes**.

Taking the Britons into partnership

The most important person in Roman Britain was the **Governor**. He probably spent most of his time in or near London – the biggest city in the province. The Governor was helped by a large staff of Romans but also relied on help from **romanized Britons**.

These were people who copied the Roman way of life, and made sure that it continued. In each town there was a council of romanized British officials. It judged law cases, made sure that corn and taxes were collected, maintained roads and buildings, and laid on sports and games for the local people.

Surviving evidence

The Romans built some very grand buildings with beautiful decorations. Some like this mosaic floor, can still be found today.

Roman villas

Most Britons lived and worked in the countryside. The richer ones lived in big, roomy farms called **villas**. The villa-owners produced everything they needed for themselves, and supplied the people in nearby towns as well. The remains of more than 600 villas, like this one at Chedworth in Gloucestershire, have been found in Britain.

The Roman historian Tacitus wrote about his father-in-law Agricola, Governor of Britain from AD 78 to 84. Here he tells us how Agricola helped to romanize the native Britons.

He encouraged them privately to build temples, public squares and good houses, and he gave them official help to do so ... He educated the sons of the chiefs in the Roman way ... The result was that instead of loathing the **Latin** language they became keen to speak it well.

Exploring further – Life in Roman Britain

To investigate daily life in Roman Britain, follow this path on the CD-ROM:
Romans in Britain > Exploring > Everyday Life
To explore a town in Roman Britain click on: The town of Calleva.

Knitting Britain together

The Romans made a major impact on the landscape of Britain. Before the conquest, the **Britons** had no solid, all-weather roads to make their journeys on. They used winding trackways that got terribly muddy in winter. The Romans had built good, straight highways all over their Empire so that their troops and goods wagons could move around quickly. Even as they were conquering Britain, they began to lay down a network of roads across the new **province**.

Thanks to this new road system, the various tribal peoples of Britain came into more frequent contact with one another. Maybe, as a result, they began to find that they had fewer reasons to fight one another, as they had often done in pre-Roman times.

Roman roads

The Romans changed the face of Britain. They built towns, cities and **villas** of stone. They laid down proper roads. We can still see many remains of these roads across Britain like this road crossing the Yorkshire Moors.

Hadrian's Wall

The Romans built Hadrian's Wall to stop raiders attacking from Scotland. They could control the people on both sides of the Wall. You can still see a lot of Hadrian's Wall today.

A passing phase?

The pirates, raiders and Anglo-Saxon settlers of the 400s AD destroyed much of what the Romans had built. The time after Roman rule in Britain came to be called the 'Dark Ages'. That makes some historians believe that – in the end – the Romans did not have much effect.

Facts and figures

Probably two to three million people lived in Roman Britain. Only one person in ten lived in the Roman towns. These people all lived **romanized** lives. So did the soldiers who defended the province and many of the local people who worked on or around the villas. But everyone else had little to do with the Romans. Most Britons kept farming in the same ways, kept wearing the same sorts of clothes, kept on living in the same sorts of huts and never learned to speak **Latin**. It is easy to forget about them, because they left so few traces of their lives behind.

Exploring further – Hadrian's Wall

The CD-ROM carries lots of pictures showing what remains of Hadrian's Wall. These remains show us what life was like on the Wall. Follow this path:
Romans in Britain > Pictures > Invasion and Warfare
Click on the pictures to make them bigger. Captions describe the pictures.

How was the grave at Sutton Hoo discovered?

In the 400s, 500s and 600s AD, many Anglo-Saxon invaders started to settle in Britain. Hardly any books have survived from that time, so it is not easy to know exactly what life was like then. The work of **archaeologists** can help here. By finding objects from the past they can glimpse what life was like.

An amazing discovery

In the summer of 1939, a group of archaeologists started digging into an ancient mound of earth at Sutton Hoo, in Suffolk. They were amazed when they found many objects that showed that it was a burial mound containing the grave of a wealthy person.

Burial ship

The archaeologists also found the shape of a whole ship, thirty metres long. Its wooden planks had rotted away but the metal nails were still there. In **pagan** times, people sometimes put ships in graves. Perhaps it showed that the dead person was about to go on a voyage to another life.

What was in the grave?

Inside the grave they found: a helmet, a sword with gold on it, a stand (possibly for holding a flag), a rod, spears, a battle-axe, a shield with bird and dragon figures on it, drinking horns with silver on them, bronze and silver bowls, a pair of silver spoons, a stringed instrument like a harp and pieces of jewellery.

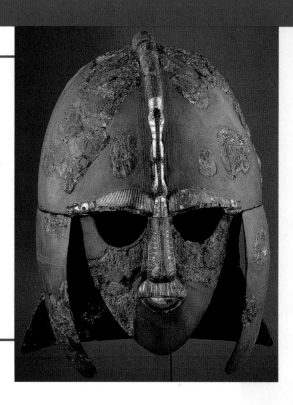

Whose grave was it?

Archaeologists found coins that were made some time between AD 620 and 640. That was in early Anglo-Saxon times. This gave them a clue to when all these goods might have been buried.

Only a rich and powerful person would have a grave like this. In the 600s, there was no big kingdom of England. Instead there were several smaller Anglo-Saxon kingdoms. Sutton Hoo was in the kingdom of East Anglia. The richest and most powerful person in East Anglia was the king himself. Some historians think the burial was made around the year AD 625. The king of East Anglia just before then was called Redwald. So was the man buried at Sutton Hoo the mighty Redwald?

Exploring further – Sutton Hoo

To find more information about Sutton Hoo click on Search on the top panel of the Contents page. Then click on Search Anglo-Saxons in Britain. Pick Sutton Hoo from the keywords on the next page and click on Enter. The screen will now show a list of pages on the CD-ROM that mention Sutton Hoo. Click on the names of the pages to find out what they show.

What was life like at the time the person in the grave was alive?

The Anglo-Saxon invaders and settlers obeyed many different chiefs. In England, the most powerful chiefs made themselves into kings. They ruled over large regions that contained mainly Anglo-Saxons, but some **Celtic Britons** too.

Anglo-Saxon kingdoms

N

Bernicia

Northumbria

Deira

Lindsey

Mercia

Wreocen-Saete

Middle Anglia

East Anglia

Magon-Saete

Hwicce

Essex

Wessex

Kent

Sussex

0   200 miles

0   300 km

Bretwalda

The most important Anglo-Saxon kingdoms were Kent, East Anglia, Essex, Sussex, Mercia, Northumbria and Wessex. Sometimes one Anglo-Saxon king would have so much power that he became overlord of all the others. The old English word for such a king was **Bretwalda**. Redwald of East Anglia was a Bretwalda in the 600s AD.

Feasting and food

Bowls and spoons were found in the Sutton Hoo grave. For rich Saxons, feasts were an important part of their lives. Kings would travel around their lands and stay at the big houses or 'halls' of their chief lords. These lords had to feed and entertain the king and his party. In contrast most ordinary people could not afford to feast on meat but made do with vegetables instead.

Worship

When the Anglo-Saxons first came to Britain, they were **pagans**. In 597 Pope Gregory the Great sent **missionaries** to Britain to convert the Saxons to Christianity. They did very well. But some people, like Redwald of East Anglia, worshipped both pagan and Christian gods.

Everyday life in Anglo-Saxon times

King Alfred the Great ruled Wessex over 200 years after Redwald ruled East Anglia. But what he wrote about his own kingdom was also true about Redwald's kingdom, 200 years before. He wrote that every kingdom had to have three different types of men. First there had to be soldiers, to keep the kingdom safe. Then there had to be monks and priests, who prayed to make sure that God looked after all the kingdom's people. And finally there had to be 'workers'. They might be craftsmen or builders, blacksmiths or jewellers. Most workers were farmers.

Exploring further – Life in Anglo-Saxon Britain

The CD-ROM contains lots of details about life in Anglo-Saxon Britain. Follow this path to discover more about everyday life:

Anglo-Saxons in Britain > Exploring > Everyday Life

If you want to find out about a topic, like work or food, you could try doing a Search. Page 19 tells you how to do this. Select the keyword for your topic.

What have we found out about who was buried in the Sutton Hoo grave?

Lots of people must have helped to make the Sutton Hoo grave – especially the burying of the ship! Can you imagine what the atmosphere must have been like? We can get some clues about it by reading an Anglo-Saxon poem, *Beowulf*. It was written down some time between the 650s and the end of the 900s. It tells the tale of a make-believe warrior, Beowulf, and his heroic deeds.

The poem is full of useful information about Anglo-Saxon warriors. In the part below – which has been put into more modern English – Beowulf has just died. This is what his people, called the Geats, did with his body before building a great mound. Did this happen at Sutton Hoo as well?

Beowulf

The Geat people built a pyre for Beowulf,
stacked it up until it stood,
hung with helmets, heavy war-shields
and shining armour, just as he had ordered.
Then his warriors laid him in the middle of it,
weeping for a lord far-famed and beloved.
In a high place they kindled the hugest of all
funeral fires... the blaze roared
and drowned out their weeping...
Then the Geat people began to build
a mound on a headland,
a marker that sailors could see from afar.
In ten days they had done the work.
What remained from the fire
they put inside it, behind a wall...
And they buried **torques** in the mound, and jewels.

Redwald

Redwald was King of the East Angles in the early 600s. Many historians believe the Sutton Hoo ship was buried for his funeral. We do not know much about him but Bede, a Northumbrian monk and historian, called him a **Bretwalda**, so he must have ruled over people outside East Anglia too. He was **baptized** as a Christian. Redwald seems to have worshipped Christ as well as the old gods. Around the year AD 616 he went to war against King Aethelfryth of Northumbria. This was to help Edwin to win the throne of Northumbria. Aethelfryth was killed in battle, so Edwin took over and became a Bretwalda too.

Other finds by archaeologists help us to understand the Anglo-Saxons. This manuscript pointer dates from about 900. It was found in Wiltshire. It is very ornate and shows us that reading and manuscripts were very valuable in Anglo-Saxon Britain.

Exploring further – Picture evidence

The picture bank (Anglo-Saxons in Britain > Pictures) shows many of the things that have survived from the time of the Anglo-Saxons. Some of the pictures show what modern artists think the Anglo-Saxons were like. Click on one of the pictures to make it bigger. A caption will tell you what the picture shows.

A Viking case study

Why did the Vikings travel from their homelands and where did they go?

The Vikings raided and settled far and wide – in Britain, Ireland, the Shetland Isles, Finland, Greenland, Iceland, Germany, France, Russia, Turkey and even Newfoundland in modern Canada. The English called them 'Danes', 'Northmen' or 'the **heathen**'. The word 'Vikings' probably comes from an old word for 'pirates'. But they were more than just pirates. In Britain they also farmed land, built towns and set up whole kingdoms of their own.

In search of a new start

The Vikings wrote very little about themselves. We cannot be sure *why* they did what they did. But writers in the lands they attacked tell us *what* they did. Some of these writers were English monks. They lived in **monasteries** full of precious things, which attracted frequent raids from the Viking raiders.

One reason why the Vikings roamed overseas was to do with land. In Scandinavia by the late 700s there was not enough farmland for everyone. Early Viking raiders saw that England had plenty of high-quality land.

Viking Norway

This is how a Viking merchant described his homeland. It was written down by King Alfred the Great in around AD 800.

... he owned no more than twenty cattle and twenty pigs, and what little he ploughed, he ploughed with horses... He said that Norway was very long and narrow. All the land fit for grazing lies along the sea-coast which is very rocky in places.

Dragonships

The sight of Viking **dragonships** on the horizon terrified people all over Europe. They had at least 32 oarsmen, and huge sails too. They cut very smoothly through water. As they came closer, the frightening figures carved on their fronts would come into view.

How did the Vikings travel so far from their homelands?

The Viking **longships** were longer and stronger than anybody else's. They could survive heavy storms at sea, but also travel up narrow rivers. 'When the Vikings felt the urge to set sail,' writes one modern historian, 'they must have felt there was nowhere in the world they could not reach.'

We know quite a lot about Viking shipbuilding methods. Sometimes important men were buried in their ships and **archaeologists** have dug up several of these ships.

Exploring further – Viking ships

Discover more about the Vikings' ships on the CD-ROM. Follow this path:
Vikings in Britain > Exploring > Discoveries, Inventions and Ideas > Amazing Sailors
Click on the pictures on the left of the screen to find out what they show.

When did the Vikings come to Britain to raid and to stay?

The Vikings first started raiding Britain in the late 700s AD. But only in the later 800s did they decide to make a full-scale invasion and settle here. We know where and when many raids took place because local monks made a record of them.

The invasion begins

In the 830s AD the Vikings raided Kent, East Anglia, and the south coast. In 851 they camped in Thanet in Kent for the winter. This was the first time they had stayed in England after the 'fighting season'. In 865 a large Viking army conquered East Anglia, Northumbria and Mercia. This was far more than a raid now. The Vikings had come to stay.

Viking warrior swords. A good sword was a family treasure, passed from father to son.

For a while it seemed that none of the English kingdoms could resist them. But under King Alfred the Great, the people of Wessex did manage to fight them off. The Vikings then stayed on in an area called the **Danelaw** – the lands they had already seized. By the 950s, however, the warrior kings and queens of Wessex took control of those lands too. Then many Vikings kept on living in this now-unified Kingdom of England.

Alfred the Great

Alfred the Great was king of Wessex from AD 871 until 899. He is the only English king known as 'the Great'. This is mainly because he managed to stop the Vikings from conquering the whole of England during their first great wave of invasion.

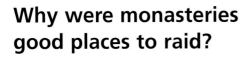

Why were monasteries good places to raid?

It is easy to see why Christian writers of the time called the Vikings names like 'the hateful plague of Europe'. They were writing in the very **monasteries** and churches that the **pagan** Vikings **plundered** for their precious things.

These places also had large stocks of food and drink, which the monks kept to give to the poor and to travellers. And monasteries were easy to attack, since the monks themselves were holy men who devoted their lives to worshipping God, not to practising the arts of warfare.

Exploring further – Alfred the Great

Follow this path to find out more about Alfred the Great:
Vikings in Britain > Biographies > Alfred the Great
In this biography, the names of Alfred's descendants, Athelstan and Edward, appear in blue. Click on the names to see details about these two kings.

What evidence is there that the Vikings settled in Britain?

In Viking times, the city of York was called Jorvik. The Vikings turned it into a busy trading centre. By the year 1000, there were about 10,000 people living there. We know quite a lot about their lives. Not long ago **archaeologists** found many of their things under a street called Coppergate.

Coppergate

The ground was wet at Coppergate so wooden and leather objects did not rot away. More finds were made in waste pits. Bits of food like the bones of pigs, sheep, deer, chickens, pigeons, and fish – plus shellfish shells, nutshells, eggshells and cereal seeds – help us to know what the people ate.

Artists and craftsmen

The Vikings were fine carpenters. The marvellous ships they built and buried show us their skill. The woodworkers of Coppergate carved wood, into items like bowls, on a **lathe** and in Jorvik also made barrels. The Vikings were also masters of decoration – carving patterns and figures on wood, stone and metal.

Guthrum

Guthrum was a Viking leader who arrived in England around AD 871. Alfred the Great defeated Guthrum at the battle of Edington in 878. They agreed that they should both rule over large parts of England – Alfred in the west, Guthrum in the **Danelaw**. Guthrum was **baptized** as a Christian and took the new name of Athelstan. He ruled in East Anglia until his death in 890.

Wessex and the Viking raiders

After the Battle of Edington, where Alfred drove back the Vikings, he continued to rule over Wessex. Meanwhile, the Vikings ruled over a large part of eastern and northern England, called the Danelaw. In the 890s new Viking raiders attacked Wessex. But now Alfred had made English defences much better and built many new **fortified** towns. Also, according to the *Anglo-Saxon Chronicle*, he 'ordered warships to be built to meet the Danish ships'. Once again, the Vikings failed to conquer Wessex.

The carving on this tombstone shows Viking warriors in action. You can see them fighting with axes. The tombstone is at Lindisfarne, one of the first places in Britain to be attacked by the Vikings.

Exploring further – Viking sagas

Much of what we know about the Vikings comes from the Anglo-Saxons, who hated and feared the Vikings. Viking sagas, or stories, can tell us about how they viewed themselves. Follow this path to explore Viking sagas:
Vikings in Britain > Exploring > Discoveries, Inventions and Ideas > Runes and sagas

Timeline

55 and 54 BC	Julius Caesar leads Roman expeditions to Britain
AD 43	Roman invasion of Britain begins
47	Maiden Castle hillfort captured
50	Roman city at London founded
51	Caratacus captured
60	Destruction of Druid stronghold on Anglesey; Boudicca's Revolt
c70s-160s	Lowland Britain becomes romanized
77-84	Governor Agricola's campaigns in north of Britain
122	Decision taken to build Hadrian's Wall to protect northern England from the Picts and Scots
313	Emperor Constantine allows Christians to worship in Empire
340–369	Time of great number of pirate raids on Britain
400–500	Picts, Scots, Saxons, Angles and Jutes invade Britain
c407	Roman soldiers withdrawn from Britain by now; end of Roman rule
476	Fall of Western Roman Empire
After 500	Anglo-Saxon kingdoms of Kent and Wessex become powerful
597	St Augustine arrives in Kent on his mission from Rome
c624	Pagan ship burial at Sutton Hoo
627	Bishop Paulinus converts King Edwin of Northumbria and his court to Christianity
635	Monastery at Lindisfarne set up
c650	Anglo-Saxon poem *Beowulf* written
after c650	Kingdoms of East Anglia, Northumbria and Mercia become dominant
731	Bede completes his *History* (a history of the English people) at Jarrow, Northumberland
793	Vikings attack Lindisfarne – beginning of Viking conquests in Britain
871–899	Reign of King Alfred the Great in Wessex
878	Vikings defeated at Battle of Edington; treaty of Wedmore
890	By now Vikings conquer all Anglo-Saxon kingdoms except Wessex
910–20	King Edward and Queen Aethelflaed re-conquer most of Viking-held lands
919	Vikings found city of Jorvik (which is now our modern York)
980	Vikings from Denmark begin new, almost yearly, raids on England
1016–1035	Cnut reigns as King of all England after new Viking conquest
1066	Anglo-Saxon English defeated at battle of Hastings by Normans, who now take over England

Glossary

Anglo-Saxon Chronicle a year-by-year history of England, written by monks – begun in the 800s and kept up till the 1100s

archaeologists people who dig up and study things from the past

baptize people are baptized with water, as a sign they are joining the Christian Church

basilica building in a Roman-built town, used for public ceremonies

Bretwalda title given to a king who was said to have power over all of Britain

Britons people who were living in Britain before the Saxon invasions

cavalry soldiers on horseback

Celtic name given to people living in Britain before Roman times; the Celts started coming to Britain from Europe around 700 BC

citizens members of the Roman Empire, protected by its laws

Danelaw land in eastern England conquered and settled by Vikings

deities gods and goddesses

dragonships Viking ships with a dragon head on the front

emigrate to leave one country and move permanently to another

empire a country has an empire when it takes land from other countries and makes the people there obey their laws

Empire (Roman) the large area of land ruled by the Romans. It covered a large part of Europe, North Africa and the Middle East.

fortified made with defensive walls and buildings as protection against attack

Governor a Roman, usually a senator, in charge of a province

heathen word used by Christians to describe non-Christians

hillforts camps in high places which were the towns of the Celts

immigrants people who come from one land to live in another

lathe tool used by woodworkers to hold and turn a piece of wood so it can be shaped

Latin the official language of the Roman Empire, used by the church and well-educated people in Anglo-Saxon England

longship Viking warship with oars and one sail

missionary person travelling to and teaching in distant lands to spread his or her religion

monastery place where monks and nuns live

pagan word used by Christians to describe non-Christians

plunder to steal goods, especially in time of war

province a territory within an empire (e.g. Britannia)

pyre pile of stuff to be set on fire, especially for burning a body

romanized following the Roman way of life

torque (also spelt torc) necklace of twisted metal, often precious

tribe a group of people often related to each other, sharing a way of life and the same leaders

villas farms with houses and outbuildings, or big country houses

woad a blue dye with which Celtic warriors painted themselves

Index

Agricola 15
Alfred the Great 21, 24, 26, 27, 29
Anglo-Saxon Chronicle 29
Anglo-Saxon kingdoms 19, 20, 21
Anglo-Saxons 7, 17, 18, 19, 20, 21
artists and craftsmen 14, 19, 21, 28, 29

Bath 5
battles 10, 13, 23, 29
Bede 23
Beowulf 22
Boudicca 10-11, 12, 13
Bretwalda 20, 23
buildings 14, 15, 16

Caratacus 11
cavalry 13
Celtic Britons 6, 8, 9, 10-11, 12, 13, 16, 20
Christianity 9, 21, 23, 29
coins 19
Colchester 12

Danelaw 26, 29
Dark Ages 17
Dio 10, 13
dragonships 25
Druids 9

emigration 4
'England' and the 'English' 7
entertainment 14

farming 17, 21, 24
feasts 20
food 20, 28

forts 6, 8, 14
Franks 7
Frisians 7

gods and spirits 9, 21, 23
Governor, Roman 12, 14, 15
graves 18-19, 20, 22, 29
Gregory, Pope (Gregory the Great) 21
Guthrum (Athelstan) 29

Hadrian's Wall 17
hillforts 8, 14

Iceni 10, 12
immigrants 4
invaders 5, 6, 18, 20, 26

jewellery 10, 19, 22
Jorvik (York) 28
Julius Caesar 9
Jutes 7

languages 8
Latin 8, 15, 17
Lindisfarne 7
London 12, 14
longships 25

Maiden Castle 8
missionaries 21
monasteries 7, 24, 27
monks and priests 21, 23, 24, 26, 27
mosaics 14

pagans 9, 18, 21
pirates 17, 24
plundering 12, 27
provinces 6, 14, 16

Redwald 19, 20, 21, 23
refugees 4
roads 6, 16
Roman bath-houses 5
Roman Empire 6, 7, 13
romanized Britons 14, 15, 17
Romans 6, 8, 9, 10, 11, 12, 13, 14, 16, 17

St Albans 12
sea-raiders 7, 24
ships 18, 25, 28, 29
Strabo 8
Suetonius Paulinus 12, 13
Sutton Hoo 18, 19, 20, 22, 23

Tacitus 10, 11, 15
taxes 14
temples 15
torques 10, 22
towns and cities 8, 12, 14, 16, 17, 29
trade 8, 14, 28
tribes 6, 8, 10, 11, 12, 14

Vikings 7, 24-9
villas 13, 15, 16

weapons 13, 19
woad 9
worship 9, 14, 21, 23
writings 8, 9, 10, 11, 15, 21, 22, 23, 24, 27